Hedgehogs as Pets

The Ultimate Guide for Hedgehogs

Hedgehogs General Info, Purchasing, Care, Cost, Keeping, Health, Supplies, Food, Breeding and More Included!

By Lolly Brown

Foreword

As with any of the first mammals, they have adapted to living life nocturnally. Although the hedgehog has thorny, spiny looking protective spikes resembling that of the porcupines', both these species are unrelated. Porcupines are a kind of monotreme and are classified as echidnas and rodents. The hedgehog got its name right around 1450 in Old England. Because people back then had noticed the creature to favor hedgerows humans came up with the animal's moniker. In fact, its name is a combination of the Middle English words "heyghoge," "heyg," and "hegge" which means hedge while "hoge," or "hogge" means pig because it had a nose like a pig's snout.

It was also known by other names like "furze-pig," "urchin," and "hedgepig" before this name, we call it up to this day, stuck. Although hedgehogs are by nature soloists and enjoy their own company the collective form of describing a group of hedgehogs is an array.

Table of Contents

Chapter One: What are Hedgehogs? 1

    Taxonomy and Scientific Name 2

    Origin & Distribution..2

    General Appearance and Behavior 3

    Physical Characteristics...7

    Senses of Hedgehogs 11

Chapter Two: Hedgehogs as Pets 21

    What Makes It a Good Pet? 22

    Pros and Cons of Owning One 28

    Hedgehog Ownership 28

    The Hedgehog as an Invasive Species 33

    Where to Purchase a Hedgehog............................34

    Popular Types of Hedgehog..................................34

Chapter Three: Preparing for Your Hedgehog 37

    Habitat Requirements 38

    Costs of the Housing Requirements....................43

    Hedgehog House Proofing 43

Chapter Four: Hedgehog Nutrition....................................45

    What they eat in the wild vs. in captivity 46

    Cat foods vs. Hedgehog foods 47

    Fruits and Vegetables 49

Hedgehog Treats 51

Toxic Foods for Your Hedgehog 52

Portions and Amounts to Feed Your Hedgehog 53

Feeding Wild Hedgehogs 53

Chapter Five: Grooming Your Hedgehog 55

How to Groom Your Hedgehog 56

Nail Trimming 58

Things You'll Need for Grooming 58

Chapter Six: Socializing Your Hedgehog 61

Behavior and Temperament 62

Owner Responsibility 63

Why do you need to socialize your hedgehog? 63

Self – Anointing in Hedgehogs 64

Chapter Seven: Breeding Your Hedgehog 67

Mating and Breeding Basics 68

Breeding Requirements for Hedgehogs 69

Housing Hedgehogs Together 70

Some Breeding Precautions 73

Chapter Eight: Keeping Your Hedgehog Healthy 75

Common Illnesses and Treatments 76

Health Tips for Your Hedgehogs 78

Human Influence 81

Chapter Nine: Hedgehog Myths, Mysteries and Fun Trivia83

Chapter Ten: Hedgehog Summary 91

    General Information: 92

    Hedgehogs as Pets: 93

    Habitat Requirements 95

    Hedgehog Nutrition 96

    Grooming Your Hedgehog 97

    Socializing Your Hedgehog 98

    Breeding Your Hedgehog 98

    Keeping Your Hedgehog Healthy 99

    Hedgehog Myths 100

Photo Credits 101

References 103

Chapter One: What are Hedgehogs?

Hedgehogs are small creatures which weigh around 600-900 grams and its span from snout to end of the tail is about 25 cm. It comes in different colored spikes with covers the topmost part of its body. It has about 6000 spikes in colors of white, brown and grey. In the presence of danger a hedgehog would roll itself up into a ball and its spines help look out for its safety. Find out a little more about our buddy, the hedgehog, in this next chapter and get to learn about its origins, lands where it is naturally occurs as well as its behaviors and traits.

Taxonomy and Scientific Name

A subfamily of the Erinaceidae in the eulipotyphla family Erinaceidae is what our feisty buddy the Hedgehog is otherwise known to be. A hedgehog is any of the seventeen species in five genera, which are spiny mammals, found in and throughout Europe. They can also be found in other continents and places such as Africa and Asia. Hedgehogs can also be found in New Zealand; however this was by way of introduction and nit natural occurrence. There was a time the Amph Echinus genus once was present in North America but it has sadly gone extinct.

Hedgehogs are not native of Australia nor do they occur in the Americas. The shews of the family *Soleidae* would be the specie which hedgehogs share ancestry with and the intermediate link between them is perhaps gymnures because this has not changed much over the span of 15 million years.

Origin & Distribution

In East Africa, hedgehogs are found across a wide range of varieties of climates and terrains. The hedgehogs of East Africa are known to have dry enclosures on good soil with enough supply of food like insects and other creatures in order to thrive. Hedgehogs are said to be abundant in

Africa, particularly in Nairobi. The weather and terrain here meets the conditions the hedgehog from East Africa needs to call a region a great habitat.

Hedgehogs can usually found in the following:

- Kenya
- Burkina Faso
- Uganda
- Zambia
- Maasai Steppe
- East Africa
- Nigeria
- Central Africa
- Kilimanjaro
- Tanzania
- Benin
- Cameroon
- West Africa

General Appearance and Behavior

The average weight of a hedgehog is approximately ½ to 1-¼ pounds and many of them have the similar size of a softball or a tad larger when they are curled up into a ball. There are some adult hedgehogs which have a slightly larger built and could weigh up to 2 pounds, which is about the size of a small guinea pig, without being overweight. Many hedgehogs are about six to eight inches in length, but it is hard to be accurate and consistent in measuring a hedgehog since their body transforms shape when it is curled up, relaxed, sitting or moving.

These little prickly guys are easily recognized because of the spines they have. These spikes are basically hollow hairs which stiffen with keratin release and used by the animal to defend itself against predators or when it feels like it is in danger. Unlike the quills of the porcupine which are barbed, poisonous and easily detached, the spines on the hedgehog do not remove easy. A young hedgehog, however, does shed its spines as it matures and is promptly replaced by adult spines. This is the process called quilling. Another reason for quilling their spines outside of growing mature ones is when the hedgehog is under extreme stress or if the animal has a disease.

The seventeen varied species of hedgehogs each have their own predators with which they have to mind and contend. Owls, ferrets and some birds prey on forest hedgehogs. On the other hand smaller hedgehog species have wolves, mongooses and foxes to fight off, dodge or succumb to. Although some of the hedgehog species are active during the day, what you want to remember is that these spiky little critters are primarily nocturnal and will be up most of the night.

In the wild, hedgehogs can be found sleeping the day away on grassy patches, under rocks and bushes. Other times they like to burrow dens in the ground. So you can see the variations of each of the species habits and behaviors, but we'll talk more about that later. Although not all hedgehogs hibernate, most wild ones do. Hibernation would also depend on species, temperature as well as food abundance. Depending on the species, our feisty little buddies are pretty vocal and like to chatter using a combination of squeals, snuffles and/or grunts.

Once classified traditionally but now belief of the hedgehog being solely an insect-eater, it has now been more apparent that our cunning little buddies are omnivorous. They are seen to favor snails, insects, toads and frogs, carrions, bird eggs, as well as snakes. Your hedgehog will not be averse to dining on grass roots, berries, watermelons, melons and mushrooms. During early spring and after hibernation, Afghan hedgehogs love to munch on berries, which constitute a big part of their diet.

The body temperature of a hedgehog can decrease to around 2 °C (36 °F) during hibernation and when the animal awakes from its state of hibernation its body temperature rises from 2–5 °C (36–41 °F) back to the hedgehogs normal body temperature of 30–35 °C (86–95 °F).

The gestation period of a carrying female hedgehog is 35–58 days but this is dependent on the species. The average yield of a larger hedgehog species is a litter of 3–4 newborns and 5–6 for the smaller ones. Like with most animal species, it is not unusual for a male adult hedgehog to kill newborn males. Hedgehogs, for their size, have an impressively long lifespan.

In the wild the larger hedgehog species has the ability to live from four to seven years and some have even been recorded to live a whooping sixteen years! The smaller sort of hedgehogs bred and in captivity lives around 5-8 years and those in the wild live up to about two to four years. A pretty impressive life feat if we were to compare it to a small mouse whose lifespan is about two years and a large rat whose lifespan can extend anywhere from three to five years.

It is the hedgehogs diet and lack of predators which both contribute to the longer lifespan enjoyed by a hedgehog in captivity. Again, depending on its size a hedgehog in a captive environment can live up to about eight to ten years. These little critters are born blind. They are also borne with a protective membrane which covers their quills and then dries up and shrinks out over the next several hours of its life. After the quills have been cleaned or when the protective membranes fall off, the hedgehog's quills emerge through their skin.

Physical Characteristics

Spines

One of the most unique and apparent physical characteristic of hedgehogs would be their spines, the weight of the spines make up for approximately 35% of the hedgehog's body weight. The unique "hairs" of a hedgehog are in fact called spines and not quills, but we often refer to the critters spines as quills.

The spines of the hedgehogs are solid shafts, unlike quills which are hollow like a feather. Additionally, the hedgehog does not let go of its spines as a form of defense, like a porcupine releases its quills. Providing another contrast between the quills of a porcupine is that the spines of a hedgehog do not possess barbs on its tips which can poke a human's skin as with the quills of a porcupine.

The spines of a hedgehog are utilized as their main source of defense. Their spines are utilized by the hedgehogs back muscles as it erects the spines in order for the spikes to point in varied directions as they criss-cross each other thereby protecting the hedgehogs skin and body.

Hedgehogs possess an orbicularis muscle which the animal contracts much like a drawstring when it curls up into a ball. The hedgehog would hide its head and legs by creating a ball and then uses its spines to protect itself.

Hedgehogs are able to puff to pop, and if a handler is poked by an individual spine it can be quite painful. Correct handling methods allow the hedgehog to become more relaxed and thereby easier to handle comfortably. The spines of the animal will lay flat toward the tail when the hedgehog is relaxed, and the spines will feel surprisingly smooth when petted from front to back.

Forehead Furrow

There is a natural region in the spines on the forehead of the hedgehog. A hedgehog would be able to raise its forehead spines if it is anxious, nervous or even mildly irritated. The furrow gives space for the raised spines so they are oriented forward instead of criss-crossing when the critter's skin is pulled down over the eyes.

Teeth

Hedgehogs roughly have around 36-44 teeth and a long, pointy snout. The first pair of incisors of the animal is a little larger than the rest of its teeth, but they are definitely not as dramatically varied in size from their other teeth like a rodent's front teeth would be. The incisors of a hedgehog do not continuously grow, not like other rodent incisors. Therefore they do not have an innate trait to chew or gnaw on objects to wear down their teeth. The baby teeth of a hedgehog are shed very early on and are replaced by rooted adult teeth. If given a poor diet this can cause tooth decay and gum disease to the animal.

Feet

Amongst the Atelerix species, hedgehogs possess 4 toes on their rear feet and 5 toes on the front feet. The nails on their front feet may require trimming a tad more frequently than the nails on their rear feet in order to prevent them from curling into the foot and injuring their footpad. The hedgehogs' feet and toes are meant to be used for walking and running. These little spikey critters do not possess opposable thumbs nor do they have fingers for grasping or vertical climbing.

Tails

Hedgehogs of both sexes possess short, stubby tails which are usually hidden under their spines. Its tail could be mistaken for a penis since is positioned on its back. The male's penile sheath and hidden penis are positioned mid-abdominally.

Fur

Our buddy the hedgehog has soft, white fur on their little faces and bellies. They usually keep their fur pristine, clean and neat and a healthy hedgehog should not display matting or caking on its fur.

Chin Mole

The hedgehogs chin mole is a small bump beneath its chin. This chin mole is both harmless and normal. It is frequently referred to as a "cutie mark."

Odor

Hedgehogs do not possess a scent gland as ferrets do and, therefore, they do not have a particularly strong body scent. The hedgehog's urine does not contain huge quantities of ammonia just like in rabbits or guinea pigs urine nor is the male hedgehog's urine stronger than the female hedgehog's urine, unlike male rats, mice, or cats.

The hedgehog does defecate and its feces do smell rank. Keep in mind that what a hedgehog eats greatly affects the odor of its feces providing a hedgehog a diet of wet foods and specific brands of foods give off more of an odor than other foods. In other words, just like us humans, the level of their gassy spells will stink according to what is fed them. There are available products, like Elimina, which are sprayed on the food or can be added to its drinking water which helps fight the gassy odor internally.

Maintaining cage cleanliness as well as choosing the proper bedding materials are important parts of keeping hedgehog odor to a minimum.

Senses of Hedgehogs

Hedgehogs, just like most other animals, utilize their senses to collect information from their environment. An interested individual who is thinking about taking care of one must take into account how hedgehogs use their senses when handling the little critters as well as during the socialization and bonding processes.

Sense of Sight

Hedgehogs' possess small, beady eyes and a very poor sense of sight. This is probably because of the fact that they have burrowing nature. It is not uncommon to find hedgehogs in shallow holes on the ground. As compared to us human beings, or even to dogs and cats, hedgehogs have quite limited binocular vision. They have a difficult time calculating depth perception and would frequently take a bad spill or fall from dangerous heights since they simply cannot tell how far they are from the ground. Other hedgehog senses are much stronger and overcompensate for this weakness in eyesight as you will soon discover in the next sections of this chapter.

Hearing

Hedgehogs sport large ears and possess a remarkable sense of hearing. Strange unfamiliar sounds or loud noises can give way for hedgehogs to react in defense by huffing and ducking their head in defense. Hedgehogs could become accustomed and can integrate into a busy household but it may take some time for the lovable creature to get used to new surroundings.

Smell

The sense of smell or olfactory system is the part of the sensory system used to smell. Almost all mammals and reptiles possess a main olfactory system and an accessory olfactory system. Although the olfactory sense in the hedgehog hasn't been studied quite as thoroughly it is not impossible but does pose a level of difficulty. Noting something more about our prickly little friend it is believed that hedgehogs and felines share the same electrical activities. Hedgehogs possess an extremely excellent sense of smell and this come in very handy and is very useful to them specially when they are in search of food and when detecting danger.

The nose of the hedgehog is moist and warm to the feel. A curious hedgehog would trim its head and snout up and sniffs the air for it to collect information from its environment and surroundings. Should it feel the slightest danger in its midst they would duck their head to protect itself. Hedgehogs detect movement or presence of strangers by the movement or noise the source makes.

Motion Detection

These little prickly critters are best at detecting any movement around them even when they are curled up into a ball, despite their poor eyesight. Unless they are completely relaxed in their environment, hedgehogs will perceive every bit of sound or movement to be a possible threat.

A hedgehog trying to go to sleep or one that is in slumber may show annoyance if movement is felt around them even though they have an idea of where the sound is coming from or they are aware of the cause of movement. You may liken it being in a dark house and you hear a sound from somewhere, this is how a hedgehog would react when it feels movement around it.

They would raise their quills when they sense movement in order to protect themselves. Hedgehogs are by nature defensive until they are sure they are safe.

It seems it is human nature to want to reach out and touch a hedgehog when it is sleeping or curled into a ball in its cage, probably because of our nature to care for something warm and living.

What we might think of touching, a hedgie may consider a poke, and it would almost always raise its quills along with a huff and a puff which could result in a prick to the poking finger. Correct handling could help avert the natural fear of a hedgie when it is being picked up.

Emotion Detection

Hedgehogs, much like other animals, are able to sense the fear, anxiousness, nervousness, or confidence of the humans who are handling them. Hedgehogs possess a tendency to react more nervously if they sense you are nervous and will relax more quickly if you are calm. This is how the hedgehog feels even your emotions and is affected by your moods and most especially you emotions.

Vocalizations

All hedgehogs are able to make a wide range of sounds that they use to talk. A caregiver of hedgehogs has to listen carefully and observe the hedgehog's behavior in order to understand clearly what your pet hedgehog is trying to say. Different pet owners can liken each noise that a hedgehog makes in different terms. Some noises require little or no attention at all on your part like when a new born hedgehog squeaks or chirps.

Now if you hear other sounds like your hedgehog clicking or popping, you should take it as a clear sign that your hedgehog is in defense mode and you will need to change the manner of how you are handling your pet hedgehog. Of course, like with any other pet, you will want to get to know your own hedgehog and identify what sound it makes and what changes are in the environment they are surrounded by to identify what is going on with your pet. Here are a few more clues on what kind of sounds a hedgehog makes.

- **Squeaking or Chirping** – this sound is frequently the first indication of new babies in a female hedgehogs nest.
- **Grunting** - this sound could be a sign of contentment.
- **Whistling or Purring** – this is a sign of contentment. A hedgehog caregiver must know their hedgehog is truly enjoying their company when they hear this sound emitted by the critter.
- **Singing** - these are strange sounds which are part of the mating ritual.
- **Huffing, Puffing, and Sneezing** – this could be a sign of irritation, annoyance, or uncertainty. You may want to find out what is going on when you hear

your hedgie make these sounds. Hedgehogs might huff and puff. You will want to take this sign that they are simply trying to tell you to back off and give them a little bit of space. Remember that hedgehogs like to be alone most of the time so don't over handle your pet.

- **Popping or Clicking** – these sounds are the aggressive and/or defensive sounds that are emitted when a hedgehog is trying to defend itself.
- **Sneezing, Wheezing, and Snuffling** – these sounds could certainly be a sign of illness. However, some hedgehogs are simply trying to have a hedgehog "conversation" with you or are simply checking things out.
- **Squealing** – A hedgie keeper could hear this sound when a fight is about to happen between two hedgehogs.It would then be a good idea to keep a close look out on the hedgies because injuries can quickly happen during fights.
- **Screaming** – This is a sound that you never want to hear. It is a sound which communicates pain or extreme fear. A fight or perhaps an accidental injury could be causes for this sound. Hedgehogs are known to make this sound in even their sleep for no apparent cause or reason; just like us humans, as if they are having a hedgie nightmare.

Defense Mechanism

There are about 6000 quills on a hedgehog and it uses them as a defense mechanism much like the porcupine does, although the spikes on a hedgehog is much sharper and harder than of a porcupine and it covers the creatures sides and back. Often times it is compared to a pincushion with needles sticking out the other ways around.

The hedgehog has the uncanny skill of rolling into a tight ball as a defense mechanism and this allows and causes all its spines to stick outward. The animals back contains two large muscles which control the position of its quills. The quills of the hedgehog protect the animal's tucked in face, belly and feet when it is curled into a ball. Its limbs, face and belly are not covered in quill but instead the areas of the hedgehog's body are covered with fur.

This manner of our spikey friend's defense is only best effective and really dependent on the number of quills the hedgehog has. Therefore as a way of utilizing its natural deterrent, some hedgehogs from the desert has evolved to become less physically cumbersome which makes them likelier to try fleeing first? When in attack mode the hedgehog will ram its spines onto their intruder. A hedgehog will stay and fight and would only roll into a ball as a last resort.

The bones of hedgehogs have been discovered in the poo-pellets of the eagle owl of Europe (the European Eagle Owl). The main predator of the hedgehog in Britain is the badger. The numbers of hedgehogs in Britain have a demonstrably lower populace in areas where there are numerous badgers. The hedgehog rescue societies of Britain will never release hedgehogs out into the wild territories where badgers are known to be numerous.

Color Variations

The hedgehog species usually sport a white face or sometimes light colored appearance. On the other hand, the Algerian hedgehog sports a darker colored face. Almost all, if not most, hedgehog kept as pets today are a hybrid of the Atelerix and Algerian species. Worth noting is that the very dark Algerian face masks are a pretty rare sort.

The spines or quills of hedgehogs can come in a range of colors in the banding. Its spines could be banded, blackish, and peach or may be a solid white.

Hedgehogs could in fact switch their color variations as they mature and get older. The best age to determine hedgehogs' actual and permanent coloration is approximately one year. Organizations like International Hedgehog Association recognize almost 100 variations of Hedgehog colors including quill colorations, white, brown, and black hedgehog varieties. The creatures quill, skin, face, nose, and leg coloration all come together into play when determining the hedgehog's real color.

A lot of hedgehog hobbyists and enthusiasts prefer to simplify the colors by entering their hedgehog wards in a number of categories. Some categories to be mentioned would be standard, or the black to brown variations, cinnicot, or the tan or light brown variations, the black eyed whites, which have 90% or more visible white quills, albinos, snowflakes, which have around 10-89% white quills, and last the pinto, which could be any color with patches of white quills.

Longevity

In the wild, hedgehogs would typically live between two to three years. Usually, the most common cause of death in the wild is because of predation and not age. In captivity, hedgehogs could live up to 10 years but those are few and far between.

Hedgehogs are much like other mammals who age faster every year. A juvenile year old hedgehog would be the equivalent of a 100 year old granny. Whilst a five year old hedgie is about seventy to eighty years old in people years. Therefore if your hedgie lives up to five to seven years, be thankful because it has lived a full life. Note though that five years is longer than the average lifespan of a captive hedgehog.

There are several factors to mind when looking at the longevity of a hedgehog. Those would be the diet it is given, the sort of bedding in its enclosure (be reminded that most illnesses come from the environment of its habitat and the cleanliness or lack of it), proper veterinary care, its surroundings and environmental stressors, and importantly, genetics. The number one and primary cause of hedgehog mortality would be various kinds of cancer. We hope that your hedge lives to a ripe old age. Unfortunately, not all pets have a long as others simply because of the previously mentioned factors.

Chapter Two: Hedgehogs as Pets

So you are really bent on getting a hedgehog for a pet, but are you ready for one? Or can you even get one, given the state of your residency? We will delve into the hedgie and its traits as a pet, the pros and cons of owning one as well as the legalities of purchasing, transporting importing and raising one in this chapter.

The world has a love-hate relationship going on with humans and hedgehogs and this has been proven time and again. A hedgie in an English garden is heaven sent and a welcome "intruder" because of how it keeps destructive insects at bay. In New Zealand, it has been deemed a pest to the insect and animal life in the regions where it was introduced. And in other places it is just down right illegal to own one and an individual in that region could face a ton of fines and an unfortunate fate for the hedgehog.

What Makes It a Good Pet?

It's an amusing little critter with many curiosities and oddities that make them all the more adorable. They are tiny enough to fit in your hand when they are small and if you are the sort who stays up most nights then a hedgehog may be the pet for you.

Hedgehogs wouldn't be what you would consider as the typical family pet, and have some special traits, characteristics and habits which do not make them suitable for some owner situations. So, it is vital to be aware and ready for some of these characteristics even before you think about purchasing a hedgehog. Hedgehogs are by nature nocturnal. If you go to bed pretty early at night, and are rushed during the mornings, it is highly likely that you will not be awake during the periods of the night when hedgehogs are at their most active. This can pose as a problem in a couple of different ways. First, when you have time and are able to play with your pet, your hedgehog will most likely want to go to sleep, which may make them quite crabby at you for disrupting their sleep time and disturbing them.

Additionally, because they are up and about while you are asleep, and if you keep the hedgehog enclosure near your sleeping area, then you would probably have a hard time sleeping because of its activities. At night, you can expect your pet to be running, shuffling, munching, and just typically be running around its enclosure as it plays and amuses itself.

Hedgehogs in fact have some very special medical needs. Hedgehog medical issues aren't terribly different than most other mammals we keep as pets. However, the methods required to examine the little prickly critters are a tad bit different. For this particular reason it makes many vets unwilling to treat them, or unsure about the correct care it needs.

If you are not ready and prepared, this may make it extremely challenging to source a vet who would be willing to meet with you. There is a high chance that they would be incapable of treating a hedgehog properly in the event of an emergency situation. It is then a sound idea to make certain that your vet will take the time to research on how to manage a hedgehog's health and how to properly care for it.

Hedgehogs are mainly scent oriented. Should you often use scented lotions, scented soaps, perfumes, or other scented products on your skin, this habit could set you up to be often nipped by your hedgie pet. Remember that hedgehogs depend on their noses to indicate to them what is food, what is danger, and what is the usual.

Should a hedgehog detect that you smell like food or anything harmlessly interesting, and then you could possibly get licked, slightly nipped, and anointed, this would make for one messy hedgehog. Should your odor smell like something which your hedgehog associates with threat and danger, your hedgehog would either be less likely to play and interact with you, or it could cause your hedgehog to bite you out of fear, which is quite different than the light taste nips.

A fear bite typically is a tight clamp down of its jaws, often hanging onto, curling and rolling around your fingers, and this can be extremely painful. Another very frequent cause of scent problems is the presence of tobacco smoke. It is very typical for breeders to get contacted by individual hedgie keepers who want to get rid of and give up the care of their hedgehogs due to the reason that they frequently and painfully bite. The hedgehog will stop their biting immediately once placed in an environment sans smoking and smokers, and when handled by individuals who do not carry the scent of smoke on their skin.

Remember never to liken your hedgehogs to dogs or cats. This sounds pretty obvious given their differences, doesn't it? But it has been noted that many individuals acquire hedgehogs expecting the little critters to behave and act as dogs or cats do. You should not expect your hedgehog to come running to you when you call out to it. You can't expect it to learn tricks, or at least not tricks that you want them to do. You can't expect them to play fetch, happily greet you at the door when you approach them. Nor can you expect them to litter box train easily.

Hedgehogs could break free and escape from their enclosures; not all of them do, but a lot of hedgehogs will sneak out from their enclosures because despite the pains you took to make sure that they are secure, there will at least be one attempt to escape from the confines of its habitat.

There are some cases where a hedgehog will make it an obviously enjoyable game of breaking out from their enclosure no matter what you do to make sure they don't and you make every attempt to secure its cage. If your hedgehog does break out of its home, you have to carefully look through your house to find it, because it would be exceedingly rare for escaped hedgehogs to come back and find its way home to you once free of their enclosure.

Hedgehogs love to munch on bugs. While they are not an absolute requirement, insects make up for a vital portion of a hedgehog's diet. If you cannot muster the idea of feeding live, captive bred feeder bugs, then you should at least make sure that you have access to a shop which sells either canned or frozen, dried insects.

Keep in mind and strongly consider the fact that hedgehogs have quills. This seems obvious. However, it is incredibly amazing how many people purchase hedgehogs, only to later give them up because how prickly these little animals are. While a correctly handled, properly socialized and amiable hedgehog will keep their quills to lay flat on their backs most of the time, once startled, given a sudden jolt to awake or otherwise if it is experiencing a bad day, even the friendliest, sweetest hedgehog will erect their quills at some point.

Don't forget, especially with baby hedgehogs that you are to be ready to find the occasional shed quill on your furniture, clothes, carpet, as well as in odd places like the toes of your newly laundered socks, inside your running shoes, the waistband of your clean, fresh underwear, your bed and blanket, and anywhere else you can think of.

It is to be noted though that hedgehog personalities and traits have improved to fit the pet qualities humans like in animals. Originally, imported hedgehogs had to be handled with gloves since the typical reaction of the hedgehog was to hiss and pop quills when in the hands of a handler. While it is notable to remark that there are still traits of this sort displayed by captive bred hedgies, the common (wild natured) personality and temperament of the hedgehog in captivity has remarkably improved to the point that, when held, would uncurl itself from a ball of needles to look around and check out, by sense, its handler and surroundings. It could also display relatively social traits at this point though it may erect its quills at the slightest change of scent sniffed, noise heard or movement detected.

At this rate, this average may continue to spike due to the fact that breeders are hard at work trying to make the temperament of the hedgehogs they breed to be more human-friendly. The downside to this is, once it makes a "successful" escape, it may not have the correct properties and traits it would need to defend itself once in the wild of the urban jungle. So, don't be too surprised to meet a hedgehog who is extremely friendly and amiable to your presence. It may even expect to be picked up, not raising it quills when so, and which would sit and calm relax on your cupped hands as it observes and considers the environment around it.

There are some who have been socialized so well that they do not even curl up into a ball or raise their quills no matter the hoopla it is hearing, sensing or smelling. Try not to let down your guard too much. You will still need to be on the lookout if your hedgehog becomes anxious, nervous or perplexed at any given situation. Don't be surprised if your hedgie becomes agitated or guarded or even outright on the defense, or even antisocial at certain given times.

It would be a wise idea to keep a journal whilst raising your hedgehog. Keep documentation of what was fed to them, how much was given, when it was given, the results of the stool. Make notations of what you used for their bedding and what works best for them and you. Take note of situations which cause them agitation and what situations they appear calm and relaxed. You will also want to note down vet visits, medicine or vitamins prescribed and given as well as illnesses it may have.

Pros and Cons of Owning One

If you are an early bird and cannot be up most nights to observe, socialize, bond and play (if it wants to) with this little prickly critter, then you may need to look elsewhere for a pet. Being the nocturnal animal that it is, it will be up most nights and will make scuffling noises as it forages for treat you have laid out for it, it could decide to get some midnight exercise and work out on its wheel, or it could just scurry around chasing its own shadow.

The upside to having one is that it does not require much in terms of housing it. It will not cost too much money to maintain it as there are readily available foods which it needs that you may already have in your cooler or pantry.

Hedgehog Ownership

There are some states in the US and municipalities in Canada where it is illegal for humans to keep hedgehog as pets and where breeders of the hedgehog are required to obtain licenses. These restrictions are the exact opposite in European countries such as Scandinavia and Italy, where it is absolutely illegal to keep hedgehogs as pets.

Some states, counties, and cities where owning, transporting or importing hedgehogs are illegal includes the entire state of California, Pennsylvania, Hawaii, and Arizona, the city of Denver Colorado, parts of New York City, and Douglas County Nebraska are places in the United States where it is absolutely illegal to possess a hedgehog. Some areas would require individuals to obtain special permits, including the states of New Jersey, Vermont, and Georgia. It is always the responsibility of the potential hedgie purchaser/keeper to check for their area's legal restrictions. By doing so you not only break the law unknowingly and you do not put a hedgehog in danger by bringing into an illegal area.

Although possessing hedgehogs is legally allowed in all of Canada and most areas and states of the United States of America, there are still a number of places where hedgehogs are deemed illegal. Below is a list including honest explanations as to why these rules and regulations are in place.

Maine

The most recent and latest information which we have gathered as of May, 2017 is the following: Two permits are required to own a hedgehog in Maine. The first is an importation permit which costs $25, and the other is a possession permit which costs $27. Presently, any hedgehog found in the State without the proper permit shall be confiscated and the owner shall be charged and mandated to pay a fine.

California

The entire state of California deems owning hedgehogs as illegal. California has put in place a law. This law states that all animals not specified and listed as legal under State law, by default, is illegal.

Only when the California's Department of Fish and Game become open to considering to listing hedgehogs under legal captive animal status, hedgehogs will be considered contraband pets and will be confiscated. These animals would either be moved out of state or, worse, destroyed.

There have been individuals who have tried to acquire hedgehogs out of state, disregarding the legalities of owning one, only to later find a number of problems. One of the issues Californians, who choose to purchase hedgehogs out of state, face is the availability of vet care. Being a responsible hedgie owner means you will have to have a vet on your speed dial should your hedgehog need medical attention. Hedgehogs are unique animals and they will need to have the specialized knowledge of a vet. If a hedgie keeper were to bring a hedgehog to a regular vet they could only give it treatment based on their knowledge of more typical animals they commonly treat, which could turn out to be detrimental for a hedgie.

Another thing to keep in mind if you live in any state of California and decide that you really want a hedgehog and consider purchasing one out of state is this; should you need to take the hedgehog to the vet, any vet you manage to contact and see may be required to confiscate the hedgehog because it is illegal to own. Moving forward after the confiscation, the hedgehog could either be moved to another state or, sadly, destroyed. The vet will also be bound and required by law to report any individual who owns or brings in a hedgehog to their clinic; this would mean that the individual who purchased the hedgehog illegally would have to face and pay California fines for breaking the rules of illegal importation and ownership of a hedgie in the state. Keep in mind, if you care enough that importing a hedgehog into California illegally puts the animal's life at risk from the onset.

Georgia

It took a while for the state of Georgia to be clear about their attitude toward owning and breeding hedgehogs. Sadly, recent information and clarity about the animal's welfare and effects on the balance of ecology in Georgia has made it clear that the state deems it illegal to own, raise, or keep hedgehogs. This is because the state is concerned that pet animals who escape may set up residence in the wild and populate.

It is odd though to find out that breeders who are able to obtain breeding licenses are allowed to flourish. However, any hedgehogs to be sold as pets will need to be transported or shipped out of state.

Hawaii

The risk of hedgehogs surviving in one of these islands are quite illegal throughout the state of Hawaii and are confiscated if authorities found them

Pennsylvania

A very unfortunate political combat has transpired within the State of Pennsylvania making hedgehogs illegal, they are illegal to the point where threats have been made against those wanting to transport hedgehogs through the state on the way to another state a great violation. All of this came about as the result of an initial and quite unusual law established in the 1990's. Under this particular law, hedgehogs within the state were legal, but it was illegal to import or transport fresh bloodlines into the state.

A number of breeders violated this law resulting in the Pennsylvania Game Commission (PGC) to declare an all-out war on all hedgehogs within the Pennsylvania state.

Homes of illegal Hedgehog breeders were raided like a major police operation. In short, owning a hedgehog in Pennsylvania under the draconian rule of PGC is very dangerous for both owner and hedgehog.

Some places where hedgehogs are illegal include:

- Some parts of New York City
- Nebraska, USA
- Ontario, Canada
- British Columbia, Canada

The Hedgehog as an Invasive Species

In regions where the hedgehogs were introduced such as the islands of Scotland and New Zealand, the hedgehog has been tagged as a pest. The hedgehog has been the culprit and cause of the extensive damage to the native New Zealand species of snails, insects, ground-nesting fowls, particularly shore birds as well as lizards. And just like most introduced species, the hedgehog lacks natural predators in these regions where it was brought.

Getting rid of the hedgehogs in these areas can be cumbersome and troublesome. Attempts to eradicate hedgehogs in the Scottish islands of North Uist and Benbecula in the Outer Hebrides rang out with outrage from the international community. Elimination of the hedgehog species in these areas commenced in 2003 with 690 killed hedgehogs. The attempt of animal welfare groups and societies to rescue the introduced hedgehogs was then promptly put in place.

Legal injunctions against the killing of hedgehogs were put in place by 2007 and by 2008 the eradication process was altered from hunting and killing the introduced hedgehogs to trapping and releasing their sort onto the mainland.

Where to Purchase a Hedgehog

It is best to ask around and find experienced hedgie keepers at this point. You will want to only deal with breeders who has good reputation and has had recent success in breeding them.

Most of the time, concerned breeders will impart with and hand over to you some of the sundries which the hedgie used during their stay with the breeders. Make sure to ask for guarantees and any paperwork which may show medical examinations, lineage, as well as proof of purchase.

Popular Types of Hedgehog

People are usually averse to choosing hybrids like the white-bellied hedgehog, the four-toed hedgehog, also known as the Atelerix albiventris and the North African hedgehog, scientifically known as the A. algirus, which is much smaller than the European hedgehog and so it is also commonly known as the African pygmy hedgehog. The long-eared hedgehog, scientifically called the Hemiechinus auritus and the Indian long-eared hedgehog, known in the science community as the H. collaris are other hedgehog sorts notably favored by hedgehog enthusiasts.

Chapter Three: Preparing for Your Hedgehog

You have to realize that hedgehogs aren't always friendly as you think they are. In fact they are mostly quite the opposite and prefer to be left to their own company rather than sharing space with another. The only time these animals would come together is when it is mating season. It was only in the early 90's when breeders started breeding hedgehogs in captivity. Due to this fact and very recent phenomena, hedgehogs are still mostly wild animals.

Habitat Requirements

Keep your hedgehog out of drafty areas and house it or them (in separate enclosures, of course, unless spayed) in a warm and well-lit location but never under direct sunlight. An indication that your hedgie may feel too warm is its nose is panting and it is pointed upward, and your pet's skin will also appear to be quite flushed.

Hedgehogs thrive best in climates ranging from 75°F and 80°F. You have to opt for a higher temperature if the temperature will be fluctuating so that the lower temperature is still within the comfort range of your hedgie. When temperatures are lower this leads to your hedgehog to eat less and notable lesser movement and activity which makes the animal more fallible to respiratory and other opportunistic infections. Temperatures ranging below 65°F could induce torpor which can be very dangerous to your pet hedgehog.

Your hedgehog has a need for heat, but temperatures too high could also be dangerous for them. It is recommended that you invest on a thermometer with a timer and one which records the high and low temps for a length of given time. This is a very useful device which is helpful in ensuring that the temperature doesn't get too high or too low without you knowing.

No matter which heating device you opt to choose and purchase you will want to make sure that your hedgie stays snug and warm. Some hedgie owners find this is a bigger challenge in the summer with air-conditioning than during the winter months.

When hedgehogs get too cold they will be likely to try to go into a form of hibernation/estivation. During this stage, hedgehogs will not eat and they become less active which can be very dangerous for your pet. The minute a hedgehog makes an attempt to hibernate it will be more likely have the same problem again in the future. And this is not a habit you want it to develop. The more constant the temperature is in its enclosure, the more beneficial for your hedgehog health and well-being.

All direct heat must be concentrated only to a portion of your hedgehog's cage. This will allow the hedgie to move to the cooler part of the cage once it gets too hot.

In case of and say there is a power outage, you should have a backup plan as to how you will maintain the warmth in the enclosure and how you will keep your hedgie toasty and comfortable. No one wants to spend their entire lifetime locked up in a tiny, cramped cage, and your hedgehog buddy is no different. As a thoughtful pet owner, you have to provide the biggest cage you can for your hedgehog. This way it has plenty of space to move in and make its own. The recommended minimum cage size is 4 square feet.

You may want to consider building a cage for your pet. Not only would it be fun, but you can provide your hedgie with a bigger cage for less money. Additionally, you can fashion your own hedgehog cage setup the way you want. Should you opt build your own cage, you would have to choose which material you want to build it out of. Typically used base materials are either metal, plastic, wood, or PVC pipe. Get busy designing, and get your creative juices pumping to come up with your own unique hedgie home design. Adapt a habitat to serve as a beautiful, comfortable home for your new pet hedgehog.

When fashion a cage, make certain all portals are small enough that the hedgehog doesn't have to squeeze through, escape but not too small that it gets stuck or injured. A wire-bottomed cage is a bad idea, lest your hedgie gets its feet caught between the mesh. A flat-bottomed cage is better because it's easier on its little feet and provides ease of patter. And finally, even though aren't normally climbers, they still can climb up on top of things in the cage to get to the top, so if you are thinking about leaving the top open, keep that in mind.

Wooden Hedgehog Enclosures

Wood is relatively easy to work with, and depending on what kind you purchase, it can be pretty affordable. You could try to scrounge up some useful, un-rotted scrap wood to build with for free, saving you a pretty penny. If you do build a cage with wood, however, be sure your wood is clean and not treated with chemicals. Also make sure there are no areas were your hedgie might get splintered.

Your self-fashioned wooden hedgehog enclosure can be as simple or as fancy as you want it to be. The most basic enclosure would involve getting hold of a circular saw because this is easier to use than a hand saw, a screwdriver and a few screws. You will also need material for the sides, like wire mesh, plastic mesh, or Plexiglas. If you opt on building a wood-based cage, you can make one out of old wood furniture. Think about re-purposing a drawer, a cabinet, or any old wooden piece of furniture into your new hedgehog's enclosure.

Plastic Hedgehog Enclosures

Plastic is an affordable choice for a DIY hedgehog enclosure. One way is to take a plastic storage bin and adapt it into a nice hedgehog cage. Remember to choose a large bin because your hedgehog will require plenty of space for itself. Think about connecting two or more bins to make a cage that has plenty of roaming space much like making a labyrinth. Mind the height of the furnishings and fittings you place in the enclosure if you plan to leave it open on the top as hedgehogs can climb up on top of what you put in the cage, allowing them reach the top and possibly get out.

PVC pipe tubes can also be used to make a strong, lightweight, and easy-to-clean enclosure. It is relatively inexpensive and available in varied diameter sizes. For a basic PVC enclosure you will need some PVC pipe, PVC cement and PVC cleaner. You can circular saw or a handsaw to cut the PVC pipe into sections. As with the wood enclosure you will also need something to make the sides; wire mesh, plastic mesh, or Plexiglas. You'll also need zip ties or a fishing line as a way to fasten the sides to the frame.

Remember that the last thing you want to put in there is its bedding. Choose the best bedding doesn't mean having to spend a lot for it. Fine saw dust could be a good choice for bedding. It is not too expensive, not difficult to find and when cleaning day comes (which is advisably once a week) you can just dump out the old bedding replacing it with a fresh one after you've cleaned out and sanitized the enclosure thoroughly.

Keep in mind that most illnesses and diseases pets in captivity acquire is based on diet and environmental conditions. Not only is giving your hedgehog the correct diet, it is equally important that you maintain enclosure cleanliness and make sure it's water bowl is checked for any contaminant (like feces or rotting food) twice every day if not more often.

Costs of the Housing Requirements

Cages bought at pet supply shops tend to look plain and uninspired. Even small store-bought cages could set you back anywhere from $45 to over a $100. Using repurposed wood will save you dollars and you would only have to spend under $20 dollars for screws and mesh. Throw in $10 more and get Plexiglass sides. PVC pipes will cost you around $35. If you do opt to use Plexiglass sidings expect to spend around $45.

Furnishings and fixtures are kept at a minimum. But consider providing your hedgie some toys to play with; a small non-toxic ball to push around, a box to hide in, a ceramic drinking bowl as well as a shallow feeding bowl. This shouldn't cost more than $15-$20.

Hedgehog House Proofing

You may want to get your hedgie out of its enclosure once in a while to give it more room and to allow it to exercise. It is best to keep your hedgehog in a confined area of the common space. Allowing it free access to the whole house is not only unwise, it is irresponsible as it could possibly get away from you; hide in place where it can't be reached or worse exit the house completely.

Get one of those collapsible mesh fences and keep it with in those walls. Make sure that it isn't low enough for it to clamber up and over. Lay newspapers in the temporary enclosure to catch any results of the call of nature.

Chapter Four: Hedgehog Nutrition

Being the nocturnal mammals they are, it is not until after dusk that hedgehogs leave their lairs to hunt and forage for food. The hedgehog rustles through fallen leaves in search of insects like caterpillars and beetles, as well as invertebrates like slugs and earthworms. Hedgehogs in the wild also like to chomp on berries and fruits, typically during early autumn when these food sources are easily available.

What they eat in the wild vs. in captivity

Hedgehogs are by nature insect eaters or insectivores, however this does not mean that you have to buy and feed your hedgehog bugs and insects alone. Surprisingly, although there are many commercial hedgehog foods out there, rarely are any of these foods suitable to nourish a hedgehog much less give it a balanced diet. What a hedgehog requires is a high protein, low-fat diet. Some good-quality cat food is a good substitute.

Pay mind that you introduce different foods one at a time. If a specific food upsets your hedgehog's stomach, this method of introduction will make it easy to identify which food is causing the upset tummy. This is also a good time to whip out your hedgie journal to record what you give it and the quantity you served.

What do Hedgehogs Eat?

The main food you have to give your hedgehog must contain a protein content of between 28%-32%. The amount of fat should be lower than 10%, and the food must contain a minimum of 4% fiber.

Bugs and Insects

Insects are the wild hedgehogs' main diet. Your hedgehog will do fine on dried cat food but adding variety to their diet is a good idea so that it isn't such a picky eater and it gets a balanced diet throughout its life. Hedgehogs are insectivores and really do love insects. Here is a short list of foods recommended for your pet hedgie to eat.

- Wax worms
- Crickets
- Beetles
- Caterpillars
- Mealworms
- Silk worms

Cat foods vs. Hedgehog foods

Cat food may be a good substitute for a hedgie to dine on but you will need to keep in mind that you will need to choose cat food which is not fish-based nor should it contain any fish elements. There are many commercially made hedgehog foods available but these rarely nourish a hedgehog appropriately much less give it a balanced diet. What a hedgehog requires is a high protein, low-fat diet

Dried or Tinned Cat or Kitten Food

If you opt to give your hedgehog cat food, do not give anything with any traces of fish or fish flavored cat food. Chicken flavor is best. Dried cat food, with no fish ingredients is preferred.

Leftover Meat

Leftover chicken and meat must be chopped into tiny pieces before being given to your hedgehog. Do not give your hedgehog raw meat, ever! Cooked, boiled, or grilled meats are acceptable, but never give it raw meat. Don't forget, fish is a big no-no.

List of fruits, vegetables, treats, and toxic foods for Hedgehogs

When in the wild, hedgies may, can, and have eaten slugs and snails. However, do not attempt to feed your pet hedgehog slugs or snails harvested from the wild. Slugs and snails can carry lungworm, which can kill your hedgehog. Best to stay away from this food sort as it may cause more harm than good to your new pet.

Fruits and Vegetables

You have to keep in mind that not all fruits and vegetables are suitable or safe for hedgehogs to eat. But here's the thing - there are so many vegetable and fruit selections which are acceptable for the hedgehog's diet. So, do take note of the ones not suitable for its diet and you and your new pet will be on a good diet track.

Fruits are softer than vegetables, so that should be alright, just make sure you avoid giving it fruits and veggies it cannot eat. Vegetables should be boiled or steamed and softened before they are fed to your hedgehog. Here is a list of the safe fruits and vegetables that you can serve up to your hedgehog.

- Nectarine
- Plum
- Dandelion greens
- Cherries
- Cucumber has little nutritional value but a lot of water content
- Strawberries and other berries
- Blueberries but do remove the skin
- Apple
- Banana

- Boiled carrot or julienne carrot because it would just be too hard when raw sweet
- Potato
- Green beans
- Melon or watermelon but all in moderation because of the sugar content
- Squash
- Pear
- Peach
- Green, red, and yellow peppers and not spicy ones
- Asparagus
- Zucchini
- Spinach
- Broccoli
- Honeydew
- Papaya
- Radishes
- Corn in small amounts

Hardly is there commercial hedgehog food which meets the nutrition requirements of hedgehogs. To recommend them could result to a sick and malnourished hedgehog. That is another thing about the beauty of keeping a hedgehog as pet; their diet is naturally available to them because humans usually have them too.

Water

Water will be just an important component in your hedgehog's diet, much like you. So be sure to provide clean water to your hedgie at all times. Make sure that you replenish its water bowl and that it is not contaminated with left-over food or feces.

Hedgehog Treats

Who doesn't like them? Scattering treats throughout your hedgehog's enclosure will encourage your pet to forage, just like it would in its natural environment. Providing small tiny surprise treats is a great way to bond with your hedgehog, but mind that you don't give your hedgehog too man. The best treats are always the ones which have some form of nutrition. Hedgehogs can become overweight and obese, so keep that in mind.

Here is a list of treats you can hide around its enclosure:

- Scrambled or boiled eggs
- Cooked rice
- Tofu
- Fruits and vegetables
- Stage 2 Baby foods - higher stages contain harmful ingredients that should be avoided

- Cottage cheese in small amounts - all other dairy products are a no-no
- Ferret treats

Toxic Foods for Your Hedgehog

There are some foods which can harm your hedgehog. There are those which can cause diarrhea, others can upset your hedgehog's stomach, and then there are some which can get stuck on the roof of his or her mouth, causing both irritation and tooth decay. The following is a list of foods you should never give to your hedgehog.

- Anything seasoned
- Anything salty
- Junk food like chips, candy, chocolate or anything sugary
- Nuts and seeds
- Peanut butter
- Dairy products other than the occasional small amounts of cottage cheese
- Fried meat
- Bread
- Fish
- Raw meat or chicken

The following fruits and vegetables:

- Garlic
- Grapes/Raisins
- Onion
- Citrus fruit and anything too acidic including oranges, lemons, limes, grapefruit, pomegranates, and tomatoes
- Dried fruit and vegetables as these can be hard to chew and digest, and may cause an upset stomach
- Avocados
- Celery

Portions and Amounts to Feed Your Hedgehog

Some hedgehogs are more active than others and will have a tendency to eat more. Hedgehogs suffering from obesity are due to large amounts of fat in the hedgehog's diet rather than over-eating. Provide your hedgehog with a wheel will lower the risk of obesity for your hedgehog. Most hedgehogs eat 1 - 2 tablespoons of food a day. Hedgehogs will stop eating when they are full.

Feeding Wild Hedgehogs

If you have a friendly hedgehog helping tend your garden and this is a welcome visitor, you can encourage it to come back by setting out some food for it. You can leave small amounts of cooked and unseasoned minced meat, fresh tinned or dried cat food or cat biscuits, dried meal worms, and some fresh water. Don't set out any bread or milk. If a feral cat, stay or pet dog, a wild fox, or raccoon is eating your friendly hedgehog's food, put the food under a ridge tile or a platform to prevent any other animals from getting to it.

Chapter Five: Grooming Your Hedgehog

Much like cats, hedgehogs are able to self-groom with very little help. However there are other aspects of having a pet hedgie that would make it more comfortable for you and your hedgie if you were to give it an occasional nail trimming. Sometimes a bath would also be in order. Hedgehogs are clean animals and work hard at keeping itself clean. Do your job as keeper of maintaining a clean cage for your pet and very little grooming should be required of you.

Hedgehogs hardly ever seek attention and most would rather be left alone, but this doesn't mean you will avoid picking up your hedgehog, even if occasionally. There are some hedgehogs like to be handled, others just don't care, and some completely dislike being touched. It really depends on your prickly companion's personality.

How to Groom Your Hedgehog

Step 1: Pick up your hedgehog gently by scoop him up from the belly. You want to feel fur and avoid its quills. Once you have it securely in your hand, you want to use your other hand to support its back.

Step 2: Stay calm and allow it time to relax. If it curls up into a ball, be patient. Keep in mind that it feels your emotions and if it should get agitated and try to explore you, keep calm.

Step 3: You need not wear gloves whilst handling your pet. Its quills may appear thorny but they are not very sharp or dangerous. You want your pet to get used to you or your odor and become comfortable around you. Just remember to be gentle. Talk to it and allow it to get used to your voice as well.

Step 4: Bedding, dirt, food remnants or other matter could get lodged in its quills, or your pet may just be plain dirty and need a good bath. You will need to get some towels and a toothbrush. A sink is a good place to give your hedgie a bath. Shampoo isn't always needed but it absolutely calls for it, your pet can have a few drops of animal shampoo in the water.

Step 5: Fill the sink with warm water (about 1 inch). You do not want to fill the sink too deep. Make sure the water is not too hot. Slowly lower your pet in the sink and wet its back gently with the warm water. Avoid getting your pet's eyes, face, and ears wet, use a moist towel instead to reach and clean these areas.

Step 6: Use the toothbrush to gently scrub its quills. Reach under it gently to wash the fur on his belly. If you used any shampoo you would want to empty the sink, replace it with clean, warm water to rinse your pet. Of course, remember to remove it from the sink whilst replacing the warm water.

Step 7: Once finished remove your hedgehog from the water, place it on a towel and wrap it up. Gently dry it and eliminate as much water as possible. A second towel will be needed if the first one gets too damp since you want your hedgie to be completely dry before putting it back in its cage.

Nail Trimming

Toenail trimming is one part of a hedgehog that often needs your attention. Since its shelter doesn't really help in wearing down your pet's nails, its nails may become sharp, and will need to be cut. The easiest tool in trimming your pet's nails is by simple nail clippers. Gently take one foot, wait for your pet to be comfortable, and then slowly and carefully trim its nails. Your hedgehog may resist at first, but be patient. The more this routine is done, the more it will get used to it.

When you clip its nails, do not clip them too deeply. If you accidentally cut the pinkish part of the nail, you can just pour some flour or cornstarch to stop the bleeding. A nail cut into the quick will bleed, so keep that in mind when clipping your hedgehog's nails.

Things You'll Need for Grooming

The hedgehog does not need too many grooming sundries and this just another bit of good news on how low maintenance it is in terms of needs. Your hedgie grooming kit should contain a pair of human nail clippers - for when it needs a good nail trimming and a few soft towels solely for its use when it needs a bath. You will need to use more than one towel for your hedgie when giving it the occasional bath as it would need to be dried out completely before going back in its enclosure.

Chapter Six: Socializing Your Hedgehog

Many experienced hedgie caregivers believe that the more time spent with an animal does not always equal a better response from an animal. Quality time tend to make a bigger impact on an animal than the length of time you spend with the animal.

The amount of time spent with an animal is important, however, what you do both do during that time is far more important. You can handle a hedgehog all you want but do it the wrong way and get nowhere in the bonding or socialization process. If you learn how to handle your pet properly and respond to its needs accurately then this will dramatically speed up the bonding and socialization processes.

Who doesn't want a mild-manned, good tempered pet? Each and every pet owner always hopes for this. Not only for their sake but also for those who will be around their pets and most specially the hedgehog itself. As previously mentioned, socialization largely depends on how a hedgehog is handled during the early stages of its life and it also depends on whether the hedgie is a rescue from an abusive home.

Behavior and Temperament

Hedgehogs are naturally shy creatures and tend to fear the unknown because even though they can easily detect motion or has a great sense of hearing they still have poor eyesight which makes these animals conscious to their surroundings and the manner of how they are being handled. When a hedgehog is anxious or fearful it will curl up and raise its spines not as a form of aggression but as a form of protection.

A new hedgie owner has to prove to their pet that they are trustworthy before a hedgehog completely relaxes with them. Ill hedgehogs will also be less responsive when handled. An uncomfortable or ill hedgie should best be left alone. An example of a natural process is quilling, this can make your pet very uncomfortable and may also affect its behavior when being handled.

Owner Responsibility

Proper handling is very important to a well-socialized hedgehog and is perhaps the most critical factor on whether or not a hedgehog will make a good pet. Hedgehog keepers need to learn and understand its subtle ways of communicating and traits so that pet owners can respond accordingly.

Owners also need to learn when to handle and how to pick up and hold a hedgehog. They need to learn what can cause a hedgehog to be scared or nervous - this is where your hedgehog journal will come in handy with your thoughtful notations of observation. Bonding with your pet is also important so that your hedgie can get used to your touch. But perhaps the most important virtue when it comes to socializing your new pet is patience, as a pet owner, this is something that is required so that your hedgie can really learn and understand what you're doing and what is expected of him.

Why do you need to socialize your hedgehog?

Correct handling of your hedgehog before you bring it home with you plays a crucial part in how your pet will bond with you and socialize with other people as well. A hedgehog which has been poked, harassed and prodded at a pet shop will likely be cranky and may not be as good of a pet as one that has been properly trained, socialized and handled by a compassionate and learned breeder.

Self – Anointing in Hedgehogs

The so – called "self – anointing" in hedgehogs occurs whenever they smell a strong scent or something unfamiliar. When this happens, this unusual behavior will make the hedgehog lick and bite the source. Once it is done with the licking, it will use it to form scented saliva then attached it to its spine using its tongue. The self – anointing among hedgehogs are actually a defense mechanism because the scent acts as a camouflage for the hedgehog and also becomes a source of poison so that when they come in contact with predators in the wild they can infect it using its infected or poisonous spines.

Another good thing to remember is the curious habit of the hedgehog which is called "self-anointing." The hedgehog when it encounters the new odor of a strange place will lick and bite the source. Then it would make a scented firth in its mouth then paste the mixture onto its spikes using its tongue. Why the hedgehog does this is still a mystery however some experts think that anointing masks the hedgehog with the new smell of the area and gives them the toxic protection they need or a source of infection for their spines to use against potential predators in the area.

Self-anointing is also called anting since the behavior is closely similar to anting habits of birds.

Much like opossums, moles and mice, hedgehogs possess a form of natural immunity against some snakes' venom through a protein in the creatures muscular system called *erinacine*. However, this is only available in small amounts and a bite of a viper could still prove to be fatal. Therefore it is known that hedgehogs, along with mongooses, pigs and honey badgers, is one of the four species of mammalian animals that have the mutation called α-neurotoxin which protect these animals against snake poison. Though it was developed separately, the four animal sorts each have nicotinic acetylcholine receptor mutations that stops the poisonous venom of snakes called α-neurotoxin from binding, this is the reason why they are somewhat immune to viper venom.

Chapter Seven: Breeding Your Hedgehog

It is crucial for every hedgehog owner, who wants to breed them, to understand the responsibility that comes with breeding these little critters. Not only will you have to think about the pairing, but after a successful mating, you will also have to care for a grumpy female but you will also need to take care of the babies.

Mother and babies will need a lot of extra, special care that will take up your time. Later on, once weaned off their mother, the babies will have to go to good homes where a responsible individual can care for them. Are you prepared for all that work?

Mating and Breeding Basics

The mating pair should not be related. They should both be mil-mannered and not ill-tempered individuals. Both should also be healthy. The age of a first time female to breed would be between 5 - 12 months. Any younger could damage their internal organs. Any older lowers their chances of conceiving.

The personality of a pregnant female hedgehog will change whilst she is laden with hoglets and more so after giving birth. Do not attempt to handle a female once she gives birth nor should keep the male stag in the cage with a female and her hoglets either, as she will have a tendency to kill or eat her array of hoglets.

You will need to handle the hoglets from day one, but you will also not want to disturb the female. It is best to find out when to handle them without giving distress to the mother. Seasoned owners find that after nursing from the mother is a good time to handle each hoglet for a little while then gently putting them back. Separate the hoglets and put them in separate cages when they are old enough for solid foods (usually on the 4th to 5th week). Make sure that you have a trusted vet on hand to call and consult in case something goes wrong with the pregnancy, birthing process, the mother or the hoglets.

When a paired mate is put together the male shall chase after her and make squealing and squeaking sounds. Try not to be alarmed as this is all part of the process. The female may respond by hissing at the male, too. There are males who will not breed when being "watched" by humans, so leave the room and give them some privacy.

Baby hedgehogs are called hoglets. A group of hedgehogs, which is rare and is only usually seen when a female gives birth, is called an array. Hedgehogs may produce litter yields ranging from 1-9 hoglets, with the average litter size being 3-4 little hoglets. The gestation period for a female laden with babies or the amount of time from conception time until birth is typically 33-35 days. The average recommended breeding age is six months.

Breeding Requirements for Hedgehogs

First and foremost, you should prepare yourself. Then once you've asked yourself all the right questions and given yourself honest answers and breeding is still on the table, you will need to prepare an adequate breeding environment.

Once you have satisfied the age and temperament requirements above, start by clearing out the male hedgehog's enclosure of knick-knacks, toys and other exercise sundries. Place the females feeding and water bowls in another corner of the male's enclosure. Once this is done, gently fetch the female and introduce her to the male's enclosure. During the 7-day female visit to the male's enclosure, you should clean out the female's enclosure to get it ready for her eventual return to her nest after the 7-day visit. Never leave the laden female with the male because when she gives birth, both parents may tend to eat the hoglets.

There are a few things that will tell you that your female is pregnant like gaining weight and a larger appetite. She will also start making piles from her bedding to make a nest for her coming hoglets.

Housing Hedgehogs Together

It is typically fine to house two female hedgehogs in an enclosure. Some females will get along, others may fight. You must first observe the female pair before leaving them on their own. Have a second cage prepared in case the females don't get along. More often than not, mothers and daughters or sisters can live together without issues. Other times, hedgehogs which got along splendidly would suddenly fight and peace is disrupted. Should you opt to house two hedgehogs in one enclosure, the habitat must possess two of everything; two food and water bowls, two litter boxes, two hiding nooks, two wheels, and so on.

When keeping a pair of hedgehogs together in one cage, you will need to make sure the cage is large enough for both. 2 feet by 4 feet wide is the perfect size and space for one hedgehog. Two hedgehogs will need double that space.

When Housing Mothers with Daughters

Keep in mind that all mothers, even hedgies go through a grumpy period after giving birth and this continues whilst their female offspring nurse. To avert the grouchiness of mum, you may want to separate them for a short period and only reintroduce the females to the mother's enclosure only to nurse. If the grumpiness continues, you may want to consider separating them for a couple of days and this may solve the problem.

Housing Two Male Hedgehogs Together

Never house two males together as they will fight and fight a lot. There have been reports of males housed together that had fought to the death. Ask your vet if spaying both males will avert this problem.

Hedgehog Quarantine Period

Quarantine is an important part of introduction of any new pet into a home, and this is the same for your new hedgie. You wouldn't be happy about seeing your old hedgie contaminated or sick because you overlooked or completely disregarded quarantine period. Each and every hedgehog have unique and specific bacteria on them which another hedgehog is probably not used to which could make the old (or new one) sick. You must avert this and not introduce those bacteria in the same cage all at once.

No matter if you bought your hedgehog from a pet shop or a breeder, you must still keep them apart for a month. Keep you two hedgehogs in different cages, and in different rooms. If this isn't possible, you must then keep them on opposite sides of the room. Wash your hands after handling one hedgehog before you handle the other. Change your shirt and other clothing that came into contact with your hedgehog before moving to the other. Wash each hedgehog's equipment separately for the first few weeks. Handle the newest hedgehog last.

Why Is Quarantine Important?

Other than what was already mentioned about illnesses, quarantine allows you 30 days to observe your hedgehog and understand what is normal for it. It usually takes this length of time for a hedgehog to get used to a new food. Quarantine also helps the pair to get used to each other's bacteria which travel through the air.

Some Breeding Precautions

Typically, hedgehogs are not social creatures. Out in the wild, they prefer live alone and it is ideal that they live that way too in captivity. However, sometimes a hedgie owner may want to house a pair of hedgehogs together and that is possible, depending on a few things. Do not, under any circumstances, house a male and female together unless each of them are spayed and neutered. Un-spayed pairs should only be left together during breeding season. Playtime must not be allowed between male and female hedgehogs, because all it takes is for you to turn your back and presto! A pregnant female!

The possibility that someone can be allergic to hedgehogs is always on the table. Dander is a typical, animal-related allergy for a number of people. Feline dander is produced when saliva is deposited on its fur during the cats' process of self-cleaning. The dander transforms into a fine dust. Most hedgehogs are usually thought to be dander free, however, they do self-anoint, which could be irritating to some human individuals, especially those who are prone to allergies.

A number of people who are allergic to small animals are in fact actually allergic to the bedding the animal has in its enclosure. Many bedding materials are dusty, but hedgehogs can be housed on many different kinds of beddings which may aid in eliminating the dust irritation. It is but a sound idea to pay a visit to a hedgehog before you close a deal and makes a purchase should you suspect you or any member of the household are allergic to other animals. It is quite possible to have red prickle marking on a handler's hands right after handling a hedgehog but it certainly isn't a consistent phenomenon.

An experienced and long-time hedgehog owner shared their hypothesis in which they theorized that when hedgehogs are extremely frightened, they could possibly emit a toxin which causes a reaction. While this certainly could explain other hedgie owner's experiences, there has never been available data or further documentation on this matter. Other experience that hedgie keepers have reported that they have had a hedgehog for quite some time and would, almost overnight, develop a sensitivity to their teeny little pet. So, no animal is really 100% allergy-free.

Chapter Eight: Keeping Your Hedgehog Healthy

It is likely for you to litter-box train your hedgehog but be ready for "accidents" as it is also likely to poop anywhere outside the cage when nature calls and it gets the urge to do so. If you do make a social area for it in your living room, for play and exercise or plain people exposure, just ensure that your floor is easy to clean.

Put away anything important that may be climbed up on and possibly get soiled so as to avoid a bigger mess. Try not to make too much of a fuss when this happens as it may agitate your hedgie, making sure that its enclosure is maintained well and cleaned regularly. As mentioned previously, most illnesses come from pathogens and bacteria which build up and thrive in dirty enclosures. Don't be the irresponsible one by not doing what is expected of any pet owner.

Make sure that you make time to check out your hedgie on a regular basis for any anomalies. Check its skin, eyes, nose, quills and body. Sudden changes in behavior could also mean that it is ailing and will need vet care. Be religious with taking observation notes on your hedgie journal to refer to when needed.

Common Illnesses and Treatments

This is where hedgehogs could somehow be likened to humans because the little prickly critters can suffer from many diseases which are common to humans including cardiovascular diseases, liver disease and cancer.

Cancer is quite typical in hedgehogs with the most common cancer being the squamous cell carcinoma but unlike in humans the squamous cell spreads very fast from the bone to the organs in hedgehogs. It is rare for a vet to recommend surgery to remove the tumors as it would require to remove too much of the hedgehogs bone structure.

A bad diet is what is believed to be the cause of fatty liver disease in a hedgehog. The hedgehog will eat foods which are rich in sugar and fat with great abandon, so a potential caregiver of a hedgehog should be aware of this bit at the onset or the hedgehog will be prone to obesity if left to its own recognizance. Hedgehogs have a metabolism which is adapted for low-fat, protein-rich insects,

Hedgehogs pass on a characteristic skin infection to their own sort as well as humans who handle them. The dermatophytosis infection, or ringworm, is caused by Trichophyton erinacei. The Trichophyton erinacei forms a distinct group of maters within the Arthroderma benhamiae species complex.

Another curiosity of the hedgehog is it adversity to a rare condition when injured or if infected. As a result hedgehogs with injury or infection become prone to bloating wherein gas is trapped under the skin and which causes the animal to inflate like a balloon. This is condition is called the balloon syndrome such was reported in 2013 by The British Hedgehog Preservation Society. According to them, there seems to be no cause for this illness or at least doctors have not yet determine it. What veterinarians do to treat balloon syndrome is to give antibiotic once the air is removed at the back of its skin after incision or aspiration. Balloon syndrome is often associated with damage in the hedgehog's lung wall or perhaps there is an external wound that causes a sort of clostridium infection.

There was another recent 2017 report by the BBC wherein the network reported the curious case of a hedgehog which inflated to a large size (about two times larger) just like a ball. According to Bev Panto, one of the head veterinarian at Stapely's Wildlife Hospital, he never had seen and experience this kind of condition throughout his career, although it may be somewhat similar to other cases he has handled but it's quite different and intriguing in its own way. He was in fact shocked because when he picked up that blown up hedgehog he thought it will be quite heavy as it appears, but it turns out that it was pretty light and full of air. Only hedgehogs suffer from this terrible condition because they're the only creatures who have the ability to curl up since they have an air space in its skin

Health Tips for Your Hedgehogs

- You, as a potential caregiver of one of these lovable creatures must make sure that its eyes are clear, free of parasites, bold, roundish, and clean. The hedgie's eyes must be wide open and should not have any watery discharge. It should also not be sunken or dull looking.

- The hedgehog's nose must be moist and clean. The nose should not show any signs of dryness, should not have any bubbly fluids, nor should it be runny.

- A healthy hedgehog's ears must be clean with no drainage, have no crustiness, or show no flaking on the outer part of its ear. Keep in mind to check its skin to make sure that there are no lumps, bare patches, abrasions, bumps, excessive dryness, or signs of mites.

- The hedgehogs' underbelly fur must not be matted. Your hedgehog's body must be filled out and muscular through the back and sides. There are some hedgehogs which have a streamlined appearance, however, their skin must not be loose or saggy and their skin must be filled out below its ribs.

- There are other hedgehogs which are plumper; however, these plumper ones must not be so fat that they cannot easily curl into a ball. A healthy hedgehog's breathing must be regular with no wheezing or indication of stress. You should not be confused with the normal hedgehog that is huffing normally.

- Take note of the quantity of food and water taken in by your hedgie from the night before and take notation if the hedgehog gained or lost a significant amount of weight. The color of hedgehog's bowel movements should be similar to the color of the hedgehog's food. Green bowel movements or diarrhea are signs of illness and stress.

- Your hedgehog should be able to move freely without limping, wobbling, or dragging its feet. A healthy hedgehog's normal gait will make a "pitter-patter" sound.

- It is widely discouraged by seasoned hedgie keeper from purchasing a hedgehog as a "rescue" in order to take it away from its horrible conditions from a breeder or a pet store. Buying the animal could improve that particular hedgehog's living conditions, however, it will do nothing to avert any future animals from being housed or kept in similar conditions.

- When you find a situation like this, gently, kindly and respectfully point out the issue of living conditions and attempt to gently educate the individual or store about correct hedgehog care. There are instances of neglect which are not intended. Instead the neglect may stem from lack of proper hedgehog care information. Should the living conditions of these animals not improve it could be necessary to let the proper authorities know of this. Hedgehog sales are governed by the USDA, which is obligated to investigate all reported issues and complaints.

Human Influence

Hedgehogs living around humans is one of the dangers most small mammals face, with cars posing as one of the greatest threats to hedgehogs as many of them, tiny as they can be, are run over as they attempt to cross roadways. In Ireland, one of the most common fatalities is hedgehogs. In just two years between April 2008 and November 2010, there was about 135 hedgehog fatalities on a total stretch of 50, 430 km. A spike in male hedgehog deaths occurred in May and June as made apparent by the significant number of male hedgehog car - cases collected.

The months when a significant increase in female hedgehog death happens during the months of June and July and notable more female deaths occurred in the month of August. Studies have suggested that these peaks were related to the breeding season for the mature ones and the exploration and dispersal of the younger ones which follows their independence.

Chapter Nine: Hedgehog Myths, Mysteries and Fun Trivia

It would please you to know the kind of impressive influence the hedgehog has on us humans in everyday life and how it has helped us see the funny side of life, the seriousness of it and all that is in between of our existence alongside the lowly but never the underdog of a buddy.

McDonald's, in 2006, transformed their design of the McFlurry cups to be more hedgehog-friendly. Before the change, sugar freak hedgehogs would get their heads stuck in the container as they tried to lick the remaining melted ice cream from inside the cup. Getting their heads stuck in the cups gave way for the poor little things to eventually starve to death, hence, the advocacy to make the ice cream cups to be more hedgehog-friendly commenced.

Here's the thing even hedgehogs in captivity seem to display this same behavior. Hedgehogs in captivity have a habit of getting their tiny craniums stuck in lavatory paper tubes. Check out hedgehog videos online and you'd see many of captive hedgehogs being filmed with a tube where their head should be. Due to this curious habit of the hedgehog considerate hedgehog caregivers have started providing their pets with clean tubing which has been cut lengthwise in order for it not to get their heads trapped. Despite hedgehog guardians proactive measures of safety it is funny to note that some hedgehogs would still knowingly to get themselves into a this curious bind once in a while. So watch out for yours when you get your own prickly pet home.

Here are other things and stories that were inspired from hedgehogs:

- Sir Richard Onslow a Parliamentarian from 1601–64 compared King Charles I of England to a hedgehog.

- Beatrix Potter's 1905 children's story The Tale of Mrs. Tiggy-Winkle has a hedgehog as its title character.

- A fantasy short story entitled "The Princess and the Hedge-pig" is the title of the short story of E. Nesbit, with can be found in the 1912 collection of The Magic World. Here a prince under enchantment and is transformed to hedgehog allowing for a curious prophecy to come to pass.

- In the chapter entitled "The Green Hedgehog," In the 1927 British detective novel The Ellerby Case by John Rhode Doctor Lancelot Priestly, the character and investigator who solved the case, is almost murdered by a green-dyed hedgehog whose spines have been impregnated with a virulent poison.

- "The Mower" by Philip Larkin wrote one of his poems on the death of a hedgehog.

- Sega first introduced Sonic the Hedgehog in 1991. Sonic the Hedgehog is the main character of Sega's video games, comic strips, and animated cartoons. It is portrayed as a blue anthropomorphic hedgehog.

- Hedgehogs may well be the second most popular animals to check out on the Internet, next to cats.

- Hedgehogs are usually solitary creatures that enjoy the company of their own shadow and would only come together during mating season. But should it come up, a group of hedgehogs are called an "array."

- The hedgehog has gained quite a following in the past decade making them one of the most sought after pets. However, there are many states in America where it is illegal to own a hedgie for a pet. States like New York City, Hawaii, Pennsylvania, Georgia, California, Arizona and Maine are states where no one is allowed to keep hedgehogs as pets.

- A hedgehog has about 5000 to 7000 quills and the animal back muscles can lower and raise its quills in response to a situation it deems threatening.

- Out of the 17 hedgehog species in the world today, none of them are native to the United States, nor are they indigenous to Australia. Hedgehogs were introduced in New Zealand and are deemed pests.

- As an adaption to their nocturnal lifestyle these little prickly critters rely on their sense of smell and hearing because they have really bad eyesight. However even their limited eyesight is best in the dark.

- The inside of the quills of the hedgehog are mostly hollow, and has a series of complex air chambers which make them light but strong. Not at all like porcupine quills which are barbed and poisonous.

- Garden hedges and the pig-like sounds hedgehogs make are responsible for how these little animals got their name, being that hedges are their preferred habitat. Hedgehogs favoring plant destroying insects make them welcome visitors to many English gardens.

- The hedgehog is one of only three animals in Great Britain that hibernate. They could, but not all of them do.

- The typical diet of a wild hedgehog is made up mainly of berries and insects, however, with their immunity to snake venom, hedgehogs aren't averse to taking down a viper and dining on it.

- The sea urchin got its name from the hedgehog. Long before getting its more adorable name which we know it today, the hedgehog was called an urchin. Thus the inspiration came about to call their unlikely counter parts from the ocean sea urchins.

- Bestiaries and illuminated texts portray hedgehogs collecting food utilizing their quills. Of course, this is an inaccurate bit of information but of the quaint portrayal the image has persisted.

- A long time ago, it was the hedgehogs that were supposedly portentous critters. However, when German settlers arrived on the shores of the United States and discovered there were no hedgehogs, the close-enough groundhog was consulted to predict the coming of winter weather.

- A serious party in New Zealand once tried to get a hedgehog elected into parliament. The votes came in and McGilly Cuddy's Party was unsuccessful.

- There was actually an Olympic Games solely for hedgehogs which included events such as floor exercises, hurdles and sprints.

- There is a lesser known tale of the Brothers Grimm about a boy who is born half hedgehog. The tale is titled "Hans My Hedgehog."

- Hedgehogs have a habit of biting and liking a new strange scent and then proceeds to make a froth mixture of the taste in its mouth with saliva after which it slathers itself with the frothy saliva on its quills. No one knows what the purpose of this habit serves.

- Hedgehogs have lousy eyesight but a real keen sense of smell. So keen is it that it can even sense the scent of a worm burrowed underground.

- There could be as many as 500 fleas which live amongst the spines of hedgehogs.
- Being the voracious eaters they are hedgehogs can wander for up to 3 km a night in search of and on the lookout for food.

- Hedgehogs are swimmers but wild ones can find themselves trapped in pools and ponds with steep sides.

- 'Pups" or 'Hoglets' are what young hedgehogs are called.

- Erinaceus which means 'spiky wall' is the Latin word for 'hedgehog'.

It has been said time and again by many experts, researchers, scientists and foodies that we humans have not even skimmed the surface of what we can and could consume. As time passed humans stopped eating many of the foods which are available to us not even considering half of what we could be potentially consuming available to us.

In many cultures hedgehogs are one food source. In ancient Egypt hedgehogs were eaten and there are some Late Middle Ages recipes which call for hedgehog meat. The hedgehog is traded and bartered throughout Africa and Eurasia to use in witchcraft and traditional medicine. Hedgehog meat, in the Middle East and especially among Bedouins, is considered to be medicinal, and is thought to cure rheumatism and arthritis.

Hedgehogs are also used and said to cure some sorts of illnesses and medical conditions ranging from tuberculosis to impotence. Inhaling the smoke of the burnt skin or bristles is said to cure fever, male impotence, and several illnesses involving the urinary tract according to most locals in Morocco. The blood of the hedgehog is also purveyed as a cure to cracked skin, ringworm and warts.

In witchcraft, the meat of the hedgehog is eaten as a remedy. The Romani people still consume hedgehogs up to this day. Whether boiled or roasted, hedgehogs are still currently served up during Gypsy dinners and feasts. The Gypsies also use the fat of the hedgehog as well as its blood for its supposed medicinal values.

Chapter Ten: Hedgehog Summary

Taking care of these prickly but adorable creatures can be a great learning experience for you and your family. Hedgehogs may seem very easy to handle and take care of because of their small size but it's actually quite harder than it looks. You have to keep in mind that these creatures are not typical pets, and there aren't a lot of people who know how to care for it properly. Make sure that you'll be committed once you purchase one, and be able to provide its appropriate needs so that he/she will be happily live with you. Take a look at some of the most essential things you need to remember in this summary chapter.

General Information:

Taxonomy: A subfamily of the Erinaceidae in the eulipotyphla family Erinaceidae

Origin and Distribution: Nairobi, Kenya, Burkina Faso, Uganda, Zambia, Maasai Steppe, East Africa, Nigeria, Central Africa, Kilimanjaro, Tanzania, Benin, Cameroon, West Africa

General Appearance:
Weight: ½ to 1-¼ pounds
Hibernation Temperature: 2 °C (36 °F)
Normal Temperature: 30–35 °C (86–95 °F).
Spine Coverage: the weight of the spines make up for approximately 35% of the hedgehog's body weight.
Teeth: Hedgehogs has 36 - 44 teeth
Feet: hedgehogs possess 4 toes on their rear feet and 5 toes on the front feet.
Tail: Hedgehogs of both sexes possess short, stubby tails which are usually hidden under their spines.
Odor: Hedgehogs do not possess a scent gland as ferrets do and, therefore, they do not have a particularly strong body scent.
Motion Detection: These little prickly critters are best at detecting any movement around them even when they are curled up into a ball, despite their poor eyesight.

Emotion Detection: able to sense the fear, anxiousness, nervousness, or confidence of the humans who are handling them.

Vocalizations:

Squeaking or Chirping, Grunting, Whistling or Purring , Singing, Huffing, Puffing, and Sneezing, Popping or Clicking, Sneezing, Wheezing, and Snuffling, Squealing, Screaming

Defense Mechanism: There are about 6000 quills on a hedgehog and it uses them as a defense mechanism

Color Variation: Its face is white/ lighter or darker in appearance; its bands are black, white or peach in color

Lifespan in captivity: 4 - 7 years; the longest recorded lifespan is 16 years

Lifespan in the wild: 2 - 4 years

Hedgehogs as Pets:

Major Advantage: The upside to having one is that it does not require much in terms of housing it. It will not cost too much money to maintain it

Major Disadvantage: It will be up most nights and will make scuffling noises.

Hedgehog Ownership:

- There are some states in the US and municipalities in Canada where it is illegal for humans to keep hedgehog as pets and where breeders of the hedgehog are required to obtain licenses.

- Some states, counties, and cities where owning, transporting or importing hedgehogs are illegal includes the entire state of California, Pennsylvania, Hawaii, and Arizona, the city of Denver Colorado, parts of New York City, and Douglas County Nebraska are places in the United States where it is absolutely illegal to possess a hedgehog. Some areas would require individuals to obtain special permits, including the states of New Jersey, Vermont, and Georgia.

Where to Purchase a Hedgehog:

- It is best to ask around and find experienced hedgie keepers at this point. You will want to only deal with breeders who has good reputation and has had recent success in breeding them.

Popular Types of Hedgehog:

- White-bellied hedgehog
- Four-toed hedgehog
- North African hedgehog
- Long-eared hedgehog
- Indian long-eared hedgehog

Habitat Requirements

- Keep your hedgehog out of drafty areas and house it or them (in separate enclosures, of course, unless spayed) in a warm and well-lit location but never under direct sunlight.

- Hedgehogs thrive best in climates ranging from 75°F and 80°F.

- The recommended minimum cage size is 4 square feet.

Ideal Types of Enclosure for Hedgehogs

- Wooden Hedgehog Enclosures
- Plastic Hedgehog Enclosures

Costs of Housing Requirements:

- Small store-bought cages: $45 - $100
- Plexiglass: $45
- PVC Pipes: $35
- Fixtures, Toys, Drinking/Feeding Bowls/ Other Cage Materials: $15 - $20

Hedgehog Nutrition

Food in the Wild: Hedgehogs are by nature insect eaters or insectivores. They usually eat wax worms, crickets, beetles, caterpillars, mealworms, silk worms.

Food in Captivity: good-quality hedgehog food or foods that has a high protein (around 28%-32%), low in fat (lower than 10%) and enough fiber (minimum of 4%).

Recommended Fruits/Veggies: Nectarine, plum, dandelion green, cherries, cucumber, strawberries, apple, banana, potato, green beans, watermelon, squash, pear etc.

Recommended Hedgehog Treats: scrambled/boiled eggs, cooked rice, tofu, fruits/veggie bites, cottage cheese

Toxic Foods for Hedgehogs: anything seasoned or salty, junk food (chips, candy etc.), nuts, seeds, peanut butter, dairy products, avocados, celery, garlic, onion etc.

Feeding Amount: 1 - 2 tablespoons of food a day

Grooming Your Hedgehog

Step 1: Pick up your hedgehog gently by scoop him up from the belly.

Step 2: Stay calm and allow it time to relax. If it curls up into a ball, be patient.

Step 3: You need not wear gloves whilst handling your pet.

Step 4: Get some towels and a toothbrush; asink is a good place to give your hedgie a bath. Shampoo isn't always needed.

Step 5: Fill the sink with warm water (about 1 inch). You do not want to fill the sink too deep.

Step 6: Use the toothbrush to gently scrub its quills.

Step 7: Once finished remove your hedgehog from the water, place it on a towel and wrap it up

Grooming Supplies:

- Nail Clippers
- Soft Towels

- Gloves
- Bathing Tub/basin
- Shampoo
- Toothbrush

Socializing Your Hedgehog

Behavior/Temperament:

- When a hedgehog is anxious or fearful it will curl up and raise its spines not as a form of aggression but as a form of protection.

- Self – anointing in hedgehogs occurs whenever they smell a strong scent or something unfamiliar; the scent acts as a camouflage for the hedgehog and also becomes a source of poison so that when they come in contact with predators in the wild they can infect it using its infected or poisonous spines.

Breeding Your Hedgehog

Sexual Maturity: The age of a first time female to breed would be between 5 - 12 months; average breeding age is 6 months old.

Baby or Young Hedgehogs: Hoglets

Array/Litter size: 1-9 hoglets, with the average litter size being 3-4 little hoglets.

Gestation Period: 33 - 35 days

Keeping Your Hedgehog Healthy

Common Illnesses: Cancer, Cardiovascular diseases, liver diseases, balloon syndrome

Health Tips:

- Always make sure that its eyes are clear, free of parasites, bold, roundish, and clean

- The hedgehog's nose must be moist and clean.

- Hedgehog's ears must be clean with no drainage, have no crustiness, or show no flaking on the outer part of its ear.

- The hedgehogs' underbelly fur must not be matted.

- Your hedgehog should be able to move freely without limping, wobbling, or dragging its feet.

Hedgehog Myths

- In many cultures hedgehogs are one food source. In ancient Egypt hedgehogs were eaten and there are some Late Middle Ages recipes which call for hedgehog meat.

- Hedgehogs are also used and said to cure some sorts of illnesses and medical conditions ranging from tuberculosis to impotence.

- In witchcraft, the meat of the hedgehog is eaten as a remedy.

Photo Credits

Page 77 Photo by user hansbenn via Pixabay.com,
https://pixabay.com/en/painting-oil-painting-photo-
painting-1826436/

Page 86 Photo by user onefox via Pixabay.com,
https://pixabay.com/en/hedgehog-sweet-hedgehog-baby-
autumn-1796136/

Page 96 Photo by user Alexas_Fotos via Pixabay.com,
https://pixabay.com/en/hedgehog-child-young-hedgehog-
1759002/

References

"16 Fun Facts about Hedgehogs" Mental Floss

http://mentalfloss.com/article/56004/16-fun-facts-about-hedgehogs

"Are you considering a Hedgehog as a pet? " HedgehogWorld.com
http://www.hedgehogworld.com/content.php

"Can You Keep Two (Or More) Hedgehogs In One Cage?" HedgeHogAsPets.com
https://hedgehogaspets.com/can-keep-two-hedgehogs-cage/

"Erinaceus europaeus" Integrated Taxonomic Information System on-line database (Retrieved July 31 2017)

https://www.itis.gov/servlet/SingleRpt/SingleRpt?search_topic=TSN&search_value=633540#null

"Handling & Grooming" HedgehogCare.com

https://hedgehogcare.org/handling-grooming/

"Hedgehog" African Wildlife Foundation

http://www.awf.org/wildlife-conservation/hedgehog

"Hedgehog" Wikipedia.org

https://en.wikipedia.org/wiki/Hedgehog

"Hedgehog Care" Hedgehog Central

http://www.hedgehogcentral.com/care.shtml

"Hedgehog Socialization" Hedgehog Headquarters

http://hedgehogheadquarters.com/secure/socialization.htm

"Indoor And Outdoor Play" Hedgehog Headquarters

http://hedgehogheadquarters.com/secure/play.htm

"Is A Hedgehog The Pet For You?" HedgehogWorld.com

http://www.hedgehogworld.com/content.php?156-Is-A-Hedgehog-The-Pet-For-You

"Physical Characteristics" Hedgehog Headquarters

http://hedgehogheadquarters.com/secure/characteristics.htm

"Sonic hedgehog gene provides evidence that our limbs may have evolved from sharks' gills" University of Cambridge http://www.cam.ac.uk/research/news/sonic-hedgehog-gene-provides-evidence-that-our-limbs-may-have-evolved-from-sharks-gills

"The Hedgehog" Notice Nature

http://www.noticenature.ie/October_Species_of_the_Month.html

"Where Hedgehogs are Illegal" Hedgehog Central

http://www.hedgehogcentral.com/illegal.shtml

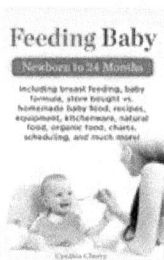

Feeding Baby
Cynthia Cherry
978-1941070000

Axolotl
Lolly Brown
978-0989658430

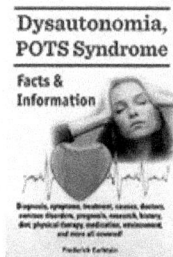

Dysautonomia, POTS
Syndrome
Frederick Earlstein
978-0989658485

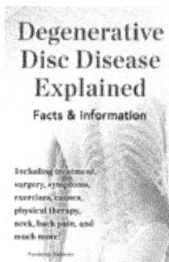

Degenerative Disc
Disease Explained
Frederick Earlstein
978-0989658485

Sinusitis, Hay Fever,
Allergic Rhinitis Explained
Frederick Earlstein
978-1941070024

Wicca
Riley Star
978-1941070130

Zombie Apocalypse
Rex Cutty
978-1941070154

Capybara
Lolly Brown
978-1941070062

Eels As Pets
Lolly Brown
978-1941070167

Scabies and Lice Explained
Frederick Earlstein
978-1941070017

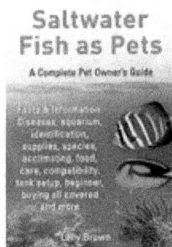

Saltwater Fish As Pets
Lolly Brown
978-0989658461

Torticollis Explained
Frederick Earlstein
978-1941070055

Kennel Cough
Lolly Brown
978-0989658409

Physiotherapist, Physical
Therapist
Christopher Wright
978-0989658492

Rats, Mice, and Dormice
As Pets
Lolly Brown
978-1941070079

Wallaby and Wallaroo Care
Lolly Brown
978-1941070031

Bodybuilding Supplements
Explained
Jon Shelton
978-1941070239

Demonology
Riley Star
978-19401070314

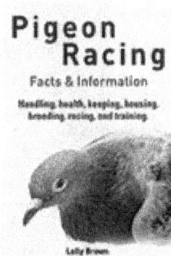

Pigeon Racing
Lolly Brown
978-1941070307

Dwarf Hamster
Lolly Brown
978-1941070390

Cryptozoology
Rex Cutty
978-1941070406

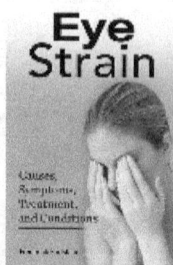

Eye Strain
Frederick Earlstein
978-1941070369

Inez The Miniature Elephant
Asher Ray
978-1941070353

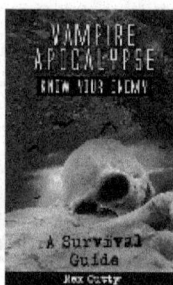

Vampire Apocalypse
Rex Cutty
978-1941070321

www.ingramcontent.com/pod-product-compliance
Lightning Source LLC
LaVergne TN
LVHW051654080426
835511LV00017B/2577